To Barb
with love and
sincere appreciation

Nancy Demme.

I Didn't Ask
To Be In This Family

I Didn't To Be In This Family

Sibling Relationships and How They Shape Adult Behavior and Relationships

ABRAHAM J. TWERSKI, M.D.

PEANUTS® *Cartoons by Charles M. Schulz*

TOPPER BOOKS
AN IMPRINT OF PHAROS BOOKS
A SCRIPPS HOWARD COMPANY
NEW YORK

First Published in 1992

Library of Congress Cataloging-in-Publication Data
Twerski, Abraham J.
    I didn't ask to be in this family / by Abraham J. Twerski : illustrations by Charles Schulz.
        p.   cm.
    ISBN 0-88687-689-3
    1. Brothers and sisters. 2. Sibling rivalry. 3. Adulthood—Psychological aspects. I. Schulz, Charles M. II. Title.
BF723.S43T94   1992
155.44'3—dc20   92-24657   CIP

Printed in the United States of America

Topper Books
An Imprint of Pharos Books
A Scripps Howard Company
200 Park Avenue
New York, NY 10166

10 9 8 7 6 5 4 3 2 1

Pharos Books are available at special discounts on bulk purchases for sales promotions, premiums, fundraising or educational use. For details, contact the Special Sales Department, Pharos Books, 200 Park Avenue, New York, NY 10166

To parents and grandparents, children and grandchildren, and brothers and sisters who love and suffer together.

Contents

Introduction // xi

1. The Problem // 1

2. First Child // 6

3. Older Sibling Domination // 26

4. Younger Sibling Domination // 41

5. Is Personality Skin-deep? // 48

6. The Transitional Object // 58

7. Addictive Relationships // 76

8. Love // 87

9. Power // 104

Epilogue // 112

Introduction

When I was a resident in psychiatric training, I was assigned the reading of Thomas Mann's *The Magic Mountain* as part of an educational program to understand human emotions and behavior via the minds of the great masters of literature.

I was deeply impressed with Mann's profound grasp of the psychological principles we were studying, and I asked my instructor whether Mann had been a physician or psychiatrist. He responded, "Don't be silly. No doctor could have that keen a sensitivity."

While professional training provides expertise in human behavior, it often does so at the cost of decreasing one's sensitivity to emotions. A surgeon cannot allow himself to be emotionally overcome by the sight of blood spurting from a severed artery, otherwise he would never get through an operation. He must be able to calmly reach for the appropriate instrument to close and suture the traumatized blood vessel. Similarly, a psychologist or psychiatrist must develop some distance from the emotions of the client, for otherwise he might be rendered totally ineffective by his reactions. These necessary barriers to empathy and reaction may dampen the sensitivity of the professional therapist. It was therefore wise to utilize the great literary works of authors whose keenness of observation was unaffected by the realistic limitations of the practical applications of psychology.

One such master of keen observation, you may be surprised to learn, is Charles Schulz, whose gift of understanding of human behavior was not fettered by the restrictions of professionalism. In two previous books, *When Do the Good Things Start?* and *Waking Up Just in Time,* I presented his brilliant insights into various psychological concepts. Comments from a number of students of human behavior and from practicing psychotherapists who are now utilizing Schulz's entertaining cartoon strips as an adjunct to therapy have confirmed my opinion that Schulz is one of the most gifted and insightful observers of human behavior known to us.

I would now like to apply his virtually uncanny ability to observe behavior and his grasp of psychological principles to a subject that can bear much enlightenment: sibling and friendship relationships. Most, if not all, of the interpersonal attitudes we exhibit in adult life have their origins in childhood. Some of our early experiences develop into positive traits, while others serve as the nucleus for distortions and misunderstandings.

Children's rational thinking does not develop as early as their emotions, hence they are often unable to correctly analyze their feelings, particularly when these are frustrated. Quite often, an emotion that is poorly understood in childhood results in an inappropriate reaction to a similar emotion when it occurs after maturity, a time when a person's rational capacity is supposed to be adequate. If we observe some of these experiences as they occur in childhood, we may be better able to understand some otherwise perplexing adult behaviors.

After looking at some sibling relationships, we will look at a variety of other childhood interpersonal experiences. As with the previous books, I believe we have here the rare opportunity of becoming psychologically more knowledgeable while being delightfully entertained.

I Didn't Ask
To Be In This Family

1

The Problem

No one doubts the influence of parents on the character development of children. The parent-child relationship was well established as the prime factor in a person's development long before Freud's epochal elaboration of the Oedipal complex and the extensive psychological literature and research on the impact of the parent-child dyad on personality formation. If one enters the word *father* or *mother* or *parent* into a psychology library computer search program, a very long list of references will emerge. If, however, one enters the word *brother* or *sister* or *sibling*, the resulting list will be comparatively scant even though a child may actually spend much more time with a sibling than with parents.

Sibling relationships have taken on an even greater significance as a result of recent social changes. For example, in the larger families of past generations, the sibling influence was diffused among probably six or seven children. In the modern two-child family, there is apt to be more interdependence and intensification of the relationship, with greater identification or de-identification. Furthermore, a woman who wishes to get on with her career may plan her family so that her two or three children are born closer together, thus allowing her to pursue her business or professional interests. These children are therefore much closer in age, in sharp contrast to the span of up to twenty years that separated siblings in families of a generation ago.

Today's mobile society has resulted in frequent uprooting of the family. Employment by a company that transfers a father to a different city every few years results in children having to repeatedly make new friends and adapt to different environments. Under such circumstances, the quest for stability is likely to strengthen the bond between siblings.

The heightened incidence of divorce has also led to siblings seeking greater security in one another to replace that which was lost by the departure of one parent. When remarriage occurs, there is apt to be further intensification of the sibling bond, as two sets of children may now share the same household, competing for space, resources, and parental attention.

As more young mothers enter the work force, more young children are placed in day-care facilities or with other caretakers. In the absence of the mother, siblings may draw closer together. And finally, changes in roles may exert an influence on sibling relationship. In contrast to the more traditional roles, wherein little girls saw themselves as becoming mothers, nurses, secretaries, or teachers, leaving the professional or executive role to their brothers, the modern little girl may be more competitive with her little brother. All these features emphasize the crucial influences that sibling relationships might have.

The relative paucity of material on sibling relationships is not due to a lack of research on the subject, but rather to the difficulty in reaching conclusions that can be applied either clinically or educationally. To understand the reason for this difficulty, just answer the following true and false statements:

	TRUE	FALSE
A child may strongly desire and welcome the birth of a younger sibling.	_____	_____

	TRUE	FALSE

A child may intensely resent the birth of a younger sibling, and indeed, the latter may result in clinical symptoms in the older sibling. _____ _____

Parents may have greater emotional investment in their first child. _____ _____

Parents may be much more relaxed with, and therefore more emotionally invested, in a second or subsequent child. _____ _____

The youngest child in the family may feel most favored because he is the recipient of everyone's attention. _____ _____

The youngest child may feel least favored because all other siblings are more senior, because he is more likely to be an afterthought or unplanned, because he is a recipient of "hand me downs," and/or because there are few movies of his early development, in contrast to his older siblings whose every move seems to have been recorded on film. _____ _____

A younger sibling will imitate and identify with an older sibling, hence this brings the two closer to one another. _____ _____

A younger sibling will try to do the opposite of what his older sibling does in order to achieve an identity of his own. _____ _____

Older siblings develop a parental attitude toward and care for a younger sibling. _____ _____

	TRUE	FALSE
Differences between the characteristics of siblings can be traced to the ways in which the parents relate to them.	____	____
Differences on how the parents relate to siblings may be traced to variations in the latter's characteristics.	____	____
A child prefers to play with a sibling rather than friends.	____	____
A child prefers to play with friends rather than a sibling.	____	____

Not only are all the above statements true, but contradictory statements may be true within the same sibling relationship, and not necessarily at different stages in their lives.

The number of variables within any given family is so great that it is virtually impossible to attribute the development of any particular trait to any single configuration or relationship. Thus, while the impact of the sibling relationship is undoubtedly considerable, this hodgepodge does not permit any neat conclusions to be drawn. "It is clear that we could 'explain' any particular combination of personalities and interests among the brothers and sisters within a family by referring to these two processes of 'identification' and its opposite, 'de-identification.'"*

Given this state of affairs, systematic scientific studies of sibling relationships offer little more in a pragmatic sense than do anecdotal observations. Each educator and every clinician is thus left to his or her own means to analyze any given situation and apply whatever dynamics appear to be reasonable.

For anecdotal observation, there is little that can equal the amazing intuitive insights of Charles Schulz.

---

*J. Dunn, *Sisters and Brothers*. (Cambridge: Harvard University Press, 1985), page 77.

"Peanuts" is a comic strip in which no adult ever appears. It is a world of children, yet, as I pointed out in my earlier books, in it we can observe much behavior that is characteristic of adults. It is a known fact that Sigmund Freud never had any direct clinical contact with children, yet many of his extrapolations on childhood, derived from observations of adults, are extremely valuable. The reverse is also possible from Schulz's observation of sibling relationships in childhood, from which we may be able to extract valuable information that can be applied to a better understanding of adult behavior, and with such data, we may be better able to understand ourselves, the people around us, and, for those of us who provide therapy and counseling, our clients as well. Furthermore, we may be able to apply some of these insights on childhood behavior when relating to children, whether as parents or as significant others.

2

First Child

What can we say about a firstborn child? Schulz, in his unique way, tells us not to generalize. Charlie Brown and Lucy are both firstborn children yet appear to be polar opposites.

As I pointed out in *When Do the Good Things Start?*, Charlie Brown and Lucy differ only superficially; basically, they both have a very low self-esteem. Charlie's poor self-image is blatant, whereas Lucy masks hers, concealing it from herself as well as others, with an attitude of superiority.

Just in case you might think Lucy's attitude is the way she really feels about herself, see what happens when she does not have to be defensive.

Incidentally, of the two adjustments to a poor self-image, Charlie Brown's is actually the healthier. Why? Because of the way he feels about himself, Charlie goes for help.

Lucy, however, is so without blemish that she would not consider getting help.

Perhaps people resist change because, like Lucy, making changes in oneself is tantamount to admitting that one was

wrong, and someone with an overinflated sense of pride will refuse to make such an admission. This is in reality a perverted sense of pride because genuine pride would stimulate a person toward self-improvement, to be the best that one can be.

In marriage counseling we frequently encounter spouses who insist that there is a problem in the marriage because the *other* spouse is wrong, and that whatever they themselves are doing is perfectly proper. In conditions such as alcoholism, the resistance to change and the refusal to accept help are the most prominent features because doing either is perceived by the person as a sign of weakness. Projecting blame onto others is a very common occurrence, and while an outside observer can readily see that blaming others is patently false, the people who are doing the blaming are convinced of the truth of their excuses.

Why should the admission that one might profit from self-improvement be so threatening? Why should accepting help be considered demeaning? Schulz has provided the answer to this

in the strip on page 8, where Lucy says to Schroeder, "You hate me, don't you?"

Lucy's know-it-all attitude is nothing but a facade to cover up a very insecure and vulnerable interior. In fact, the more vulnerable one is on the inside, the greater the fortification of one's protective facade. It might seem absurd to assert that people who are loudest in the proclamation of their perfection are precisely those people who have the most intense feelings of *inferiority*, but that is indeed the way it is. The ability to ask for help is an indication that one's self-esteem is not at the lowest possible point, because one at least feels good enough that asking for and accepting help is not a threat to his or her ego. This is why Charlie Brown, who seems to be so pathetic a character, is actually healthier than Lucy. Furthermore, by asking for help, Charlie has the opportunity to grow (assuming that he finds a psychiatrist other than Lucy), whereas Lucy, who might superficially appear to have a better sense of self-esteem but who rejects help, is unlikely to achieve much personality growth.

What are some of the factors that might be involved in a firstborn's developing feelings of inferiority? For starters, he or she is not only the smallest member of the family unit, there being no one younger, but there is no one who is even close to the same size. Father and mother are giants, as are grandparents, uncles, and aunts. A laterborn child, even though he or she is now the smallest, has at least a sibling who, while bigger, is not a towering giant in whose presence one feels completely dwarfed.

The firstborn child may be the one who suffers the greatest degree of displacement. Until a sibling arrives, a firstborn child receives all the parental love and attention. This is abruptly and drastically diminished when a sibling appears on the scene. The

latter does not share the parents equally with the older sibling. Because an infant needs so much more care, it receives the lion's share of parental attention. The older sibling may not be able to interpret this situation correctly, and may feel that the parents favor the baby over him or her.

Anticipation of the birth of a sibling can generate anxiety, and older siblings may act out this anxiety with aggression toward the pregnant mother or other siblings. As we have seen, despite the attitude of superiority Lucy portrays, she is really quite insecure. Hence she acts out her resentment toward the impending newcomer to the family by taking it out on Linus.

Linus, on the other hand, having been totally dominated and subjugated by Lucy, has taken refuge in his security blanket and is oblivious to the pregnancy.

Children of Linus's age are observant, often acutely so, and the pronounced change in mother's physical configuration hardly escapes being noticed. There has probably been abundant talk about the expected addition to the family, as well as preparation of the nursery to accommodate the baby. That an otherwise observant child can be oblivious to all of this can only be due to something that prevents the child from coming to the obvious conclusion.

Denial of the obvious is generally due to its being in some way threatening. To Linus, who has been crushed by Lucy, the advent of a new baby means the loss of much parental attention and relinquishing the preferred status of being the youngest child. As we will soon see, this event also presents an opportunity for growth in self-esteem. How do people deal with a challenge that can be interpreted either positively or negatively?

Some people rise to the occasion and cope with the challenge to their advantage, others choose to escape. As we will soon see, the blanket is to Linus what alcohol is to the alcoholic. Linus retreats to the security of his blanket and makes himself oblivious to the entire event.

Instead of being a threat to one's ego, the arrival of a baby may result in the older sibling's identifying with the parent, and thus experiencing an increase in status. It is a rare occasion when Charlie Brown jumps for joy, and the advent of a younger sister, which gives him a feeling of seniority, is an occasion for celebration.

Linus's comment to Lucy is right on target. As we noted

earlier, Charlie's low self-esteem is of the variety that encourages growth, whereas Lucy's grandiose attitude precludes any growth. Lucy, therefore, never would have reacted to a baby sibling the way Charlie did.

Sometimes we may have observed a person's reactions and said, "Gee, am I ever glad I don't react that way." However, there are times when observing another person's reactions should make us think, "I wonder why I didn't react like that?" This can stimulate a self-examination that may be very profitable in promoting character growth.

In this instance, Charlie is right. Status seeking need not always be seen as an undesirable motivating force. Many explorers, scientists, and pioneers in their respected fields have been at least partially motivated by a desire to elevate their status. When these actions result in actual achievement, such motivation need not be discouraged. On the other hand, when one seeks status with something that contributes nothing to anyone's betterment, it is indeed an empty and worthless pursuit that is nothing but an ego trip.

People may be driven by status seeking to lead community drives to provide for the homeless or to take up the causes of the underprivileged. More power to them! If they boast of how many people they have helped, they deserve the recognition. But if all they can boast about is having sat at the same table with the mayor or governor, something that does not help anyone, forget it!

Schroeder is wrong. An autographed baseball is in no way similar to caring for a younger sister.

Loneliness may well be the most distressing feeling to which a person is subject. Granted, being an only child allows one to be the center of attention and the focus of all parental love and care. But Charlie understands that surrendering this uniqueness is a small price to pay for no longer feeling the distress of loneliness.

Loneliness can occur in many ways. Some people who have made it to the top, whether as executives, professionals, or politicians, will admit that they long for the days when they were less prominent—and far less lonely.

As our egos push us to reach the top, we ought to keep in mind what it will be like once we get there, and give serious consideration as to whether the prominence is worth the price.

Lucy, of course, cannot conceptualize this. Given her need for predominance, anything that would distract from her is a threat.

An older sibling may see in the younger sibling someone who is going to admire him and perhaps emulate him, and this may enhance his self-esteem.

How often do we hear a proud father say of his son, "He's a chip off the old block"? The greatest compliment you can give a woman is to tell her that her charming and talented daughter is "so much like her mother."

While flattering comments may indeed contribute to one's self-esteem, words are but words. A much greater impact is made when someone emulates another person. To see one's ideas or actions adopted by someone else is tangible testimony that one is being appreciated.

I have observed many instances where partners in a marriage have diverse customs and practices, and the profound salutary

effect on the relationship that occurs when one spouse adopts the practices of the other. Trivial as these may be, their adoption by the other spouse is a validation of one's values.

I have dealt with the clinical problem of low self-esteem in some of my writings (for example, *When Do the Good Things Start?*). Both therapists and laypeople often ask about techniques for elevating someone's self-esteem. One of the most effective ways, when this is possible, is to *do* something that will in some way validate the other person.

For Lucy, however, a Charlie Brown with self-esteem would be devastating, since this would deprive her of her prime vehicle for expressing her attitude of superiority.

There is an old saying, "What makes a small child happy? Seeing someone smaller than oneself." A child who is dwarfed by the adults that surround him may feel so insignificant that he is thrilled to encounter someone he is taller than (apologies to my English teachers for ending a sentence with a preposition). This has its behavioral counterpart in adults. Some people will assuage their low self-esteem by associating with people they can easily identify as being inferior to them. However, if no one in

their environment suits this purpose, they may disparage others in order to feel superior to them.

Lucy's need to deride Charlie Brown confirms our thesis that her grandiosity is but a facade to conceal her feelings of inadequacy. She is thus threatened by anything that would make Charlie Brown less of a subject for her derision.

If you are tempted to make a derogatory remark about someone, stop and think about the reason for the remark. You may be revealing how little you think of yourself.

The possibility that Charlie Brown's self-esteem might be enhanced by having a younger sister is so threatening to Lucy that she resorts to drastic measures to avert it.

One of the strange phenomena sometimes observed in the family of a recovering alcoholic is that the sober spouse, who may have complained bitterly about the partner's drinking, may actually sabotage the recovery. One woman who participated in a family support group said, "If my husband had tried to get sober before I joined Al-Anon, I probably would not have let him. His drinking enabled me to be in charge of the family finances, hold the keys to the car, and be the authority in the

family. If he had tried to get sober before I received the help I needed, I would not readily have relinquished my status, and I would have somehow done something to precipitate a relapse." If the sober spouse could achieve a good sense of self-esteem on

her own, she would not need her husband's drinking to give her the status of being superior to him. Lucy would not need to deflate Charlie Brown if she felt better about herself.

Since Lucy's self-esteem has not improved, she continues to knock Charlie Brown, and unfortunately, her wish comes true. Perhaps just as a matter of the natural course of Charlie Brown's severe inferiority feelings, or because Lucy has helped intensify them, Charlie Brown relapses into his characteristic attitude.

Charlie Brown's inferiority feelings are greatly intensified when his attempts to gain some status are defeated.

Lucy is now going to try and help Charlie Brown feel better. Sometimes people who purport to help may actually increase the damage. For example, if a student who has good potential happens to fail a course, he could be helped to see just why he was unsuccessful, and how he can eliminate the obstacles to success. He can thus be encouraged to try again. However, when someone gives him "helpful" advice to try something that is less challenging and more in keeping with his limited capabilities, his feelings of inadequacy are aggravated rather than relieved.

Charlie Brown still tries to salvage something out of being an

older brother, but Lucy will not let him succeed. People who have low self-esteem are very apt to generalize, and when they find that one person thinks poorly of them, they assume everyone else does, too. Charlie Brown interprets Lucy's rejec-

tion of his offer to tell about his little sister as being typical of what he can expect from others.

Here Schulz's acute insights are again evident. Despite Charlie Brown's feelings of inadequacy, he is not a quitter. Even after repeated losses on the ball field, he continues to try to win. As I have pointed out, Charlie actually has more personality strengths than Lucy, who can never admit a failure, because this would totally decimate her.

When Charlie Brown's efforts to gain status via his little sister prove unsuccessful, he becomes depressed, but he does not go down in defeat. Rather, he musters his strength to claim an identity of his own.

There is something of Charlie in many of us, and we may sometimes try to impress other people in various ways. If this should fail, we would be wise to learn from Charlie Brown and find legitimate pride within ourselves.

*R*esentment toward a younger sibling does not necessarily require a rational basis. Or to put it another way, the threat of loss of parental attention and the need to share parental love with someone else *is* a rational basis for resentment. At any rate, such resentment may occur even when there are abundant resources for both children.

This may be the point of the biblical story of Cain and Abel. According to the account in Genesis, these two siblings were in line to inherit the entire world from their parents, the only other humans in existence. Cain could have said to Abel, "I'll take the northern hemisphere and you take the southern," or "I'll take the eastern hemisphere and you take the western." There was more than enough space to comfortably accommodate both. But no, rivalry broke out and ended with the older sibling killing the younger one.

Does this mean that sibling rivalry is universal and inevitable? Probably not. If the older sibling does not feel threatened by the advent of the younger sibling, rivalry need not occur. Indeed, as we saw with Charlie Brown, he welcomed rather than resented his younger sibling, because rather than being a threat to him, he perceived her as enhancing his self-esteem. Even if the

younger sibling is not perceived this way, but the older sibling
feels good enough about himself and feels secure in maintaining
parental love, resentment is not as apt to occur.

Resentments are thus most likely to occur where there exists a void, as when one feels a loss of parental love. In his unique way, Schulz shows this with Lucy's remark that her resentment of Linus occurs only when she is otherwise dissatisfied—that is, resentment would not occur if she were content, as would be the case if there were something good on TV.

Siblings tend to organize themselves into twosomes, and in families where there are three children, two are likely to form a special bond, leaving the odd one out.

This may establish a pattern that is repeated in adult life. For example, it has been noted that when a group of three is confined within a finite space for an extended period of time, an alignment of two against one often occurs even when all three had previously been friendly to one another.

A possible explanation for this phenomenon is that in every relationship there are apt to be conflicting feelings. There may be some things we dislike in people of whom we are otherwise fond. In a dyad relationship, the negative feelings may be totally overlooked, perhaps because one feels impotent to act on them, or because one values the advantage of the relationship, and this

precludes focusing on the negative features that would undermine it. When a third party enters the picture, one may form a bond with the third person and feel empowered to act on the negative feelings. Or perhaps the formation of a bond with the third person makes the former friendship dispensable.

The "pairing" creates a new unit, a "team" as it were. Especially for people who have had difficulty with a personal identity, the emergence of a new entity, the *team*, allows them to acquire a feeling of importance as a member of the group, a feeling they had not been able to achieve as individuals. Most of us can probably remember the formation of gangs in elementary school. The target of the gang was immaterial, serving only as a focal point to unite a group of kids who were otherwise dissatisfied. Sadly, this trait often persists into adulthood, as manifested by street gangs, whether on a small scale in city streets or on a larger scale in community and world politics.

Linus has been the underdog. The awareness that the younger sibling might be a "rerun"—that is, fashioned after him and hence someone with whom he may easily form a bond—results in elation for Linus. By the same token, this realization is devastating to Lucy, who sees the new twosome entity as formidable.

The "ganging up" phenomenon of early childhood may be the prototype for the factionalism that occurs in society, such as political parties or pro- and anti-this or that. While social factionalism generally persists, the intrafamilial diverseness is often left behind as children grow up. Socially, the diverseness is set aside when the larger group is threatened as a whole, as when a country unites to fight an enemy, or a community pulls together to cope with a natural disaster such as a flood or earthquake. In the case of the family, its members tend to close ranks and form a more cohesive unit in order to cope with the various challenges and stresses of everyday life.

3

Older Sibling Domination

MADAM ABSOLUTELY, THERE
IS NO DOUBT, FULLCHARGE

*O*lder siblings often exercise their seniority by assuming a domineering role. If the older sibling is placed in a caretaking position, with implied delegation of authority by the parents, this domination is overtly encouraged. However, even when the age gap is not great, the older sibling may totally subdue the younger.

Younger siblings may defer to older ones as to a parent, respecting them for their superior wisdom. Yet while accepting parental guidance serves as a model after which submission to appropriate authorities is patterned—for example, civil or ecclesiastic authorities, something that is necessary for participation in organized society—deference to a sibling who is just a bit senior may be the prototype for unquestioned acceptance of others' opinions.

How many people will vote for candidate X simply because a friend told them to, or will suspend their own judgment and allow themselves to be led by people with questionable qualifications? Furthermore, these people may defend their position with vehemence even though they have not the slightest idea what the issues are.

We should learn from Linus to examine some of our convictions. We might just discover that we are quite ignorant about some of the certainties we embrace. A more critical examination of some of our convictions might eliminate such sources of error.

Younger siblings may develop conflicting attitudes. On the one hand, they may be adamant and even defiant of older siblings, asserting their total independence. On the other hand, reality may dictate that they accept their dependency.

Conflicting attitudes toward authority is hardly a novelty. Some primitive cultures are known to have created deities to worship only to subsequently demolish them. In modern times, we do much the same with political figures, first elevating them on pedestals, then putting them through humiliation. This may very well be a consequence of the dependence-independence conflict wherein the reality of being dependent necessitates relating benignly to a superior in order to avoid being rejected, while the anger at being dependent may result in resentment toward the one upon whom one feels dependent.

While Linus is vigorously independent, his attitude changes dramatically when he must face his limitations.

In many ways, our lives are regulated by laws—how fast we may drive, what rate of interest we may charge, what rights of others we may not violate, and so on. Yet most of our behavior is not regulated by laws; rather, it is determined by social influences. We are indeed free to make decisions within the confines of the law, but in reality this freedom is quite curtailed by social pressures.

In our growth and development, submission to the law is primarily modeled after parental authority, whereas allowing our behavior to be determined by social pressures has its origin in sibling domination. Society determines what is "appropriate," and failure to comply with socially dictated standards may arouse a sense of guilt.

This difference between the two types of compliance may be

seen in payment of union dues or political dues on the one hand, which is generally done to secure one's job, versus donating to a charity or a community drive on the other hand. Although no punitive action follows failure to donate to a charity, the guilt that this would engender is no less powerful an incentive than the threat to one's security.

Religion can be a powerful influence in regulating human behavior. Whereas legislative controls generally have some rational basis and may be amended at society's behest, this is less true of religious rules, some of which are dogmatic in nature and to which many people defer, although they may express

their displeasure over accepting infringements on their comfort.

We often accept what we think is "rule by the wise," which would indeed be to our advantage if the "ruling wise" were indeed wise. Sometimes we defer to those we accept as wise for no other reason than they have asserted that they are indeed wiser than we are, although this is often highly questionable. How many people truly believed the Vietnam War was a just war simply because they assumed the president and his advisors had more knowledge than they did?

Of course, even in a civilized society, brute force remains a powerful determinant of behavior. Brute force may be in the shape of actual physical violence, or it may be manifested by threatening one's means of livelihood or destroying one's reputation or standing in the community.

The various social pressures may not only dictate one's behavior, it may also mold one's attitude. There have been numerous instances in history wherein a population that initially objected to the ideology of a despot eventually came to believe that what they had been ordered to do was ethically and morally correct.

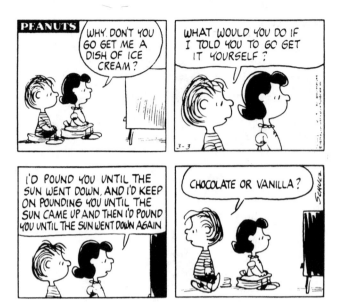

Although some doubt as to the new ethics may persist, the subjugation by a greater force may be so absolute that one loses faith in one's own judgment, and instead of challenging an incorrect ideology will surrender to it. Many people in fascist or Communist countries may have initially disagreed with the party line but subsequently became its adherents. This is the ultimate crushing of the spirit that has repeatedly occurred in totalitarian societies.

In many situations where we feel ourselves dominated, we may try to reach a compromise. Sometimes this works, and we can score some points for ourselves. Not infrequently, the superior force is so overwhelming that little, if anything, is conceded, and the terms of the negotiations are so heavily in favor of the superior force that the compromise is anything but that.

This reality may make its first appearance in dealing with a domineering older sibling; its counterpart in society can be seen in international negotiations or, on a more individual level, when dealing with the IRS. Many people would paraphrase Linus that the "IRS is all of the time."

Yet being the underdog is not always hopeless. Every so often, little Davids vanquish the mighty Goliaths. A taxpayer in possession of a letter from the IRS with a favorable ruling on a particular question may be able to win in an audit, and even politicians, who are notorious for backsliding on their campaign promises, may face dire consequences if they renege on an important commitment. While it is too often true that brute force triumphs, there are enough instances where right is triumphant over might to make life livable. In such instances it is most amusing to observe the frustration of the vanquished Goliaths, who react as so elegantly stated by Lucy, "You drive me crazy."

Although some people in positions of power believe that they will remain there unto eternity, others realize that one day they will be deposed. Many despots have thus squirreled away vast fortunes in anticipation of the day when they will be over-thrown. Officials in elected positions may be aware that they may one day lose an election. Victims of domination may be able to exploit this vulnerability to their advantage.

Many people in political office have an Achilles' heel, and

some have had their careers dismantled by people of far less stature who were able to expose these weak spots. For example, possession of a photograph of a candidate in a compromising position or knowledge of a moral or ethical lapse has been as effective in dismantling a career as a pair of pliers in Linus's hands.

Although we may have little sympathy for people who have aspired to and have attained positions of power and now find themselves totally frustrated, we might find it within our hearts to have a bit of compassion for a president who finds himself

handcuffed by Congress. For us common folk, giving up a project that is unmanageable may be unpleasant, but it is not formidable. Many people have given up unsuccessful careers and tried their luck elsewhere. Businessmen have declared bankruptcy and subsequently went on to be successful at other ventures. But where can a president go to give up?

In contrast to the domination of a younger sibling as exemplified by Lucy, an older sibling may assume a parental role, with caregiving and compassion as exemplified by Charlie Brown.

What determines whether an older sibling becomes tyranni-

cal like Lucy or caregiving like Charlie Brown? One factor may be the self-esteem status of the older sibling. As we have already seen, Lucy's self-esteem is more fragile than Charlie Brown's, hence she is extremely self-centered and cannot give of herself at all. Charlie Brown is an example of the family member who seeks to enhance his self-esteem by becoming a caregiver.

Although Charlie Brown's caregiving adaptation can occur in any family, this is particularly apt to occur in families where one or both parents are dysfunctional and, due to parental default, one of the siblings assumes a parental role. In today's society, where both parents may be employed, the caregiving role may fall to a sibling even though there is no parental dereliction. The parental role is assumed by the sibling who, for whatever reason, feels it necessary to enhance his self-esteem. This is often, but not always, the oldest sibling.

Some children may have an overactive sense of responsibility, and they hold themselves responsible for all problems that occur in the family, even assuming that if there is parental discord it is because they are somehow not good enough. These children

become the "fixers," and try to maintain peace and equilibrium in the family. This trait often persists into adult life, with these people choosing an occupation that allows them to fulfill their caregiving needs and role as helpers, such as nurses, social workers, doctors, and teachers.

There is nothing intrinsically wrong with this adaptation, and indeed, some of the finest providers of human services were childhood "fixers." However, problems may arise when they are unable to fulfill this role, as when some disability interferes with their capacity to perform. They are then apt to fall into deep depression, since they are deprived of their only source of self-worth. A problem may also arise when the "fixer" enters into a marriage where he or she is the caregiver for the spouse. A man may be attracted to a woman for whom he sees himself as the provider and caretaker. Should this woman attempt to assert herself and develop a career of her own, the husband may feel threatened by losing his role as provider, and the relationship may deteriorate. Similarly, a woman who chooses a husband who allows her to fulfill a maternal role may inadvertently

do things that encourage the husband to remain subordinate. Not infrequently, wives of alcoholics unwittingly contribute to persistence of the alcoholism by taking on the role of being the responsible person in the family, something to which they may have become accustomed in childhood. To fulfill their caregiving needs, they give a tacit approval to the husband's irresponsibility.

Although caregiving fulfills a need for the "fixer," it may also elicit resentment, and the constant expenditure of energy and devotion of one's time encroaches on one's freedom to do things for oneself. However, relinquishing the role of "fixer" may give rise to feelings of guilt and, in particular, a loss of self-esteem since the feeling of worthiness has been contingent upon providing service to others.

Alert parents may detect such tendencies in their children and can help them by (1) not asking them to take on more duties than they should realistically bear; (2) helping them realize that they are not at fault for adversities that occur within the family; and (3) helping them feel that they are loved and worthy independent of their being "fixers."

The resentments that the caregiver may harbor as a result of being imposed upon may convey themselves, even nonverbally, to those for whom they care, and this may result in a reaction to their resentment, guilt being one of the more common ones.

In adulthood, people may refuse legitimate help because of the guilt engendered by being cared for. Thus, being cared for excessively by an older sibling—or for that matter by a parent—may result in two opposite adaptations. The person may remain overly dependent on others in adult life, or may become fiercely *in*dependent and reject help even when it is appropriate. Providing just the right amount of care is one of the greatest challenges in parenting.

The caregiver may be a loser all the way, since he may never be able to satisfy the expectations that he has taught others to have of him, nor can he fulfill his own needs and aspirations because of the constant demands on his energies. Anyone who has experienced this disappointment will easily identify with Charlie Brown.

Lucy intends to maintain her superiority throughout life and is not the least bit upset by the fact that Linus is emotionally crushed.

As we shall see a bit later, Linus seeks refuge in his security blanket, an escape we can hardly begrudge him. Lucy gives lip service to eventually relinquishing her dominating role, but Linus knows better. "Lucys" do not change their personalities that easily.

4

Younger Sibling Domination

Although domination by an older sibling is more common, it is not unusual for the opposite to occur. The younger sibling may be brighter, wittier, more verbal, more outgoing, or the gender preferred by the parents. Especially if the age gap between the two is not great, the seniority can be overridden by factors that give the younger sibling the upper hand. In the case of Charlie Brown, he is older than Sally, but poor Charlie has been a loser from the start.

Once this negative self-image sets in, and this may occur very early in life, the child may behave in a manner that conforms to this self-concept, which results in repetitive failure, thereby reinforcing the low self-esteem. Unless something occurs to interrupt this pattern, this negative self-image may persist into and throughout adulthood.

Obviously, Charlie Brown is not in any way defective. We would certainly not be amused by the repeated misadventures that befall a child who has a handicap. Charlie Brown's failures amuse us precisely because Charlie is in fact a perfectly normal, bright youngster. Somehow, Charlie has developed profound

feelings of inadequacy that are totally unwarranted by fact, and he operates according to his self-image. Charlie loses at everything because he believes himself to be a loser, and the reason we laugh at him is because we can identify with him. We, too, often make self-fulfilling prophecies, and if we fail, it is often because we believe we will fail.

Charlie is clearly much brighter than Sally,

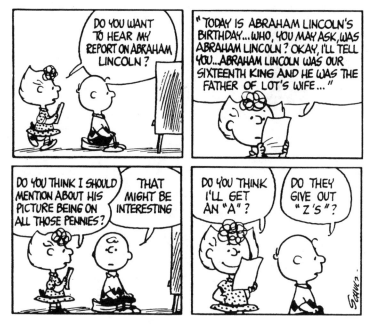

yet Sally has found ways to dominate him. Although she is younger, she exploits her brother's negative self-image to achieve this domination.

It is not unusual to find siblings harboring contradictory attitudes. Thus, although Sally knows that Charlie is brighter than she, she acknowledges this only with the greatest reluctance. Sally was the recipient of Charlie Brown's caregiving, and some people may be resentful of those who help them. This may be so because they are uncomfortable with feeling obligated, or because they feel guilty for having imposed on them. They may react to this resentment by assuming an attitude of superiority, thereby essentially denying their indebtedness. In order to achieve and maintain this attitude of superiority, they may belittle the person to whom they feel they are indebted.

This maneuver to deny one's indebtedness may be a factor in adolescent rebellion against parents. Parents who have sacrificed much for a child are totally bewildered when the child turns against them and accuses them of gross abuse. This mechanism is also evident in instances where, say, a wife supports her

husband through professional school only to be abandoned in favor of another woman.

To people who are the beneficiaries of others' kindnesses I would say, "Acknowledge a favor. No one asks you to be eternally indebted, just to be civil and decent." To people who wish to do acts of benevolence I say, "Do so if you think it is the right thing to do, but do not expect a return. In this way, you will be spared disappointment."

Guilt is a potent tool, and it is often used to manipulate others. This tactic may begin in childhood and is often manifested by adults. Parents may unwisely try to control their children by guilt. "If you marry that boy/girl and I die of a heart attack, you will have to bear that guilt for the rest of your life." Not only is this cruel and unfair, it's also counterproductive.

Sally indeed gets her way, but Charlie's attitude is hardly loving.

While there are various factors that bring about divisiveness among people, a powerful unifying force is being threatened by a common adversary. At such times people bury their differ-

ences and join forces in a common defense. This, too, can be seen in childhood. Siblings who had been at each other's throats may be brought closer together when a parent remarries and a new family is brought into the home. "My" anxiety is converted into "our" anxiety, and the desire to dominate a sibling is set aside in favor of building an alliance.

Sally wishes to achieve the ultimate victory of acquiring her

older brother's room, but the realization that she, too, may ultimately be forced to leave the parental home generates so much anxiety that she elects to drop the entire issue and forgo the triumph.

Would it not be wonderful if humanity could set aside personal ambitions and unite against a common "enemy"? If we could only realize that injustice, poverty, and hatred are destructive to all of us, we could forgo some of our desires for triumph and join hands in what we should realize is self-survival. Like Sally, we might be initially lured by the prospect of triumph, but if we only learn from history what Sally learns from Charlie—mainly, that the conqueror is eventually conquered—we might give up the thought of pursuing personal gain at the expense of others.

5

Is Personality
Skin-deep?

*O*ne of the issues that has never been completely resolved is that of nature/nurture. The occurrence of physical characteristics, such as eye color and blood type, has been quite accurately elucidated in terms of genetic factors. In regard to less tangible characteristics, such as emotional makeup and behavior, the full story is as yet unknown. Conventional wisdom holds that behavior is learned rather than inherited. Yet there are some studies that have convincingly demonstrated genetic influences even on behavior and emotion. Even without formal studies, many people who have observed newborn infants who have not yet had any exposure to environmental influences state that different "personalities" are detectable.

As I have already mentioned, I believe that Charles Schulz writes primarily to entertain, yet his intuitive insights into psychological matters are sometimes uncanny. I have heard it said that the difference between an artist and a nonartist is not in the former's greater manual dexterity but in that person's accuity of observation. In other words, the reason artists can draw so well is because they *perceive* things differently than a nonartist. This may be true of writers and cartoonists as well. They may possess a more accurate or profound power of perception that they then translate into the written word or graphic symbol.

Although you are undoubtedly most familiar with Snoopy, there is an entire beagle family in the comic strip, and the lesser-known siblings, in decreasing order of frequency of appearance, are a brother Spike; a brother Marbles; and a sister, Belle.

Snoopy is Schulz's version of Walter Mitty. Throughout the strips, Schulz masterfully demonstrates various aspects of negative self-image problems. In Charlie Brown, the negative self-image is manifest in his overt feelings of being a failure. Lucy reacts to these feelings with an attitude of superiority and conceals her feeling of inadequacy by dominating everyone, although her underlying feelings of inadequacy do emerge at times.

Snoopy is an example of yet another adaptation: flight into fantasy. If one is unsatisfied with one's role in reality, one may develop a compensatory identity in fantasy.

This can also happen in an extreme form in psychosis, where a person imagines himself to be a king or the messiah. In psychosis, the flight into fantasy is a one-way street, where the individual remains trapped in the fantasy world and is unable to adapt to reality. In nonpsychotic conditions, the flight into fantasy is temporary, and the individual does return to reality.

Snoopy realizes that as an animal who exists in a civilized world dominated by human beings, he is "low man on the totem pole." He also knows that he is totally dependent for his sustenance on the "round-headed kid." Snoopy has rather few accomplishments of which he can be proud. He is quite timid, being terrified of the cat next door. Nor does he fulfill the purpose of protecting the home from intruders, a function that is often expected of a dog.

Snoopy craves recognition, but, alas, it is not readily forthcoming. Not having the opportunity to be a leader among his peers, he seeks recognition elsewhere.

Some people seek association with those who are socially inferior so they can act superior. While some highly qualified leaders have had the position of leadership forced upon them, others have sought positions of authority in an effort to compensate for their own feelings of inferiority. Thus, Snoopy becomes the leader of a group who are far beneath him in size and strength.

In his fantasy world, Snoopy avoids the constraints of reality.

There can be various adaptations to unwarranted feelings of inadequacy. For example, some people with very intense feelings of inadequacy, who anticipate being rejected by everyone, may isolate themselves from others, because if one does not associate with others, one cannot possibly be rejected.

We have seen how Snoopy periodically escapes to his world of fantasy. Yet he does essentially live in reality and associates with Charlie Brown, Lucy, Linus, and Sally. Snoopy's brother Spike, however, is a bit worse off. He not only lives in a world of fantasy, he has completely withdrawn from contact with other creatures.

Some psychologists have postulated that a psychotic may hallucinate in order to escape from his terrible loneliness. If his condition has caused him to break off communication with the

outside world, he may carry on a conversation with imaginary voices or even with himself.

Like Snoopy, Spike flees into a fantasy world, but unlike Snoopy, Spike virtually loses contact with reality. In his fantasy world, cactuses become sentient beings.

Another of Schulz's amazing insights is evident in his description of Spike. While guilt feelings may often be healthy, as when a person feels guilty for having done something that was indeed wrong, it is also possible to have guilt feelings that have no basis in reality. For this kind of guilt, no amount of penance is effective, because one has not done anything for which forgiveness is in order. I have seen a number of patients in therapy who were referred by their clergy because they continued to have guilt feelings that were not relieved by absolution.

When people have guilt feelings that are unrelated to an actual misdeed, they are apt to conjure up some act for which they feel guilty in order to make some sense of why they feel this way. They may seize upon some trivial act in the remote

past or fabricate a misdeed. Since this is a distortion of reality, it fits well into the scheme of psychosis.

There is an element of paranoia in many cases of psychosis,

and we see this in Spike's reference to being persecuted by coyotes.

These two siblings then, Snoopy and Spike, share the psychological reaction of escaping from reality into a fantasy world, although they do so in two distinct ways.

Belle, the only female in the family, appears to be radically different. She has a regular job, appears to be firmly rooted in reality, and shows no signs of escaping into fantasy.

Why is Belle so different from her brothers? This difference may be attributed to either nature or nurture. Obviously, the genetic makeup of a female is different from that of a male, and we also know that there are some personality characteristics that are gender-linked. Or perhaps Belle's personality is different precisely because, as a female, she is subject to different environmental influences. We cannot draw any conclusions from Belle as to why she is more reality-oriented than her two brothers.

But here comes Marbles, the third male sibling in the family.

Marbles is radically different from either of his brothers. He has no idea whatever of a fantasy world and is completely unable to understand Snoopy.

The difference between Spike and Snoopy is that because Spike has totally broken off from the outside world, he has taken up permanent residence in his fantasy world. While Snoopy periodically retreats into fantasy, he does come back. Yet if Snoopy had been fully occupied with living in reality, he would not have needed any fantasy life at all.

Daydreamers tend to be people who, for whatever reason, are dissatisfied with reality, so they are less occupied with reality. These people are likely to be the "quiet one" in the family.

Why is Marbles so different? Can it possibly have something to do with the fact that, in contrast to Snoopy and Spike, Marbles is spotted?

It is intriguing to speculate on this. Embryologically, a fetus develops from three layers of primitive tissue: ectoderm, mesoderm, and entoderm. The digestive tract and its associated

organs are of entodermal origin, muscles derive from the mesodermal layer, and the *skin* and the *brain* are of ectodermal origin. This is why viruses that affect the skin are also those that might affect the brain, as is evident in measles encephalitis and chicken pox encephalitis. It is thus possible that siblings who share skin features are more likely to share personality traits. Hence Marbles being spotted may be a clue as to why he is so different in character from his unspotted brothers.

I doubt if this was even remotely considered by Schulz, who may never have even heard of ectoderm. But the Schulz genius lies in his acute perceptions and his intuitive grasp of nature, with the ability to translate these insights into his entertaining comic strip characters.

In his book *The Sleepwalkers*, Arthur Koestler describes some of history's greatest geniuses, whose epochal discoveries advanced scientific knowledge even though they were largely oblivious of the magnitude of their discoveries. Schulz may rank

alongside them, and this is why I have been fascinated with studying the psychological principles that are contained within many of his otherwise entertaining strips.

6

The Transitional Object

*L*et us now move on from childhood sibling relationships to other childhood experiences that may impact upon adult behavior.

Upon emerging from the mother's womb, the infant experiences the first of many increments of deprivation of comfort and security. During its intrauterine existence the child is totally enveloped in warmth and experiences no hunger, thirst, or environmental changes. As the infant separates from the mother, it begins to experience these discomforts, but it is fed frequently and is fairly often cradled in parental arms. As the child grows, there is a progressive withdrawal of direct parental contact and nurture, and the child may try to compensate for these losses by attachment to an object or objects. This object is referred to as a "transitional object," in that it provides a bridge between the infantile state of dependence to the mature state of independence and self-sufficiency. As a child matures, he or she should gradually wean itself and detach from the transitional object and develop a state of greater or lesser independence. It is possible, however, that instead of detaching, the growing individual may simply substitute other objects for the transitional object.

Relatively few people, even as adults, ever achieve a state of total independence. The dependency of adult life is usually diffused among spouse and/or family members, friends, and God. On the other hand, the dependency might be quite similar to the intense attachments of childhood. When the object of attachment is alcohol, a drug, or food, we recognize the condition as an addiction.

The attachment to a transitional object in childhood does not necessarily foretell a dependent state in adulthood, since the growing child may resolve the dependency needs as he or she matures. Failure of such resolution, however, may result in the persistence of an attachment into adult life. While the most familiar transitional objects are things such as dolls, teddy bears, and security blankets, which, as inanimate objects, may provide the constancy and stability the child craves, it is possible that older siblings may serve as transitional objects, provided they are willing to subordinate their needs to those of the younger sibling. Moreover, this attachment to a sibling as a transitional object has been seen to extend into adulthood in personal relationships that take on an addictive quality. Although they are not as constant and controllable as inanimate objects, older siblings have the advantage of better representing the parent whose attention has been withdrawn.

In the following illustration, Peppermint Patty is overcome by anxiety over the inevitable separation from her parents and reaches out for support to Charlie Brown, who, though not a sibling, happens to be the only one around and thus serves as an acceptable transitional object.

This is an excellent example of the desperate nature of seeking escape from the anxiety of abandonment, and helps us understand that the choice of a transitional object may be quite irrational. As Schulz has amply demonstrated, Peppermint Patty does not hold Charlie Brown in high esteem and, in fact, berates him both to his face as well as to others, including Charlie Brown's father. Yet when threatened by the prospect of abandonment, even Charlie Brown suffices as a transitional object.

As anyone who has observed a child's relationship to a transitional object knows, the attachment can be most intense. The child may refuse to eat or sleep if the object is not immediately at hand, and may cry incessantly until it has been returned. When the transitional object is a teddy bear or a blanket, it is relatively easy to pacify the child, but if it's a sibling who is unable to satisfy the child's demand for constant presence, the child may exhibit frustration.

While there are differences between inanimate and animate objects of addiction—primarily that the former is completely passive while the latter can react—there are sufficient similarities so that an understanding of the course of addiction to one provides valuable insights into the other.

A child's attachment to a transitional object should not be misinterpreted as resulting from parental dereliction or failure to provide adequate love and care. There are realistic restraints on a parent's time and energy—household duties, job, attention to

other children—so that the child's demands may be beyond what the parent can satisfy.

The similarities between childhood attachment to a transitional object and adult dependencies are striking. In depicting Linus's attachment to his "security blanket," Schulz has provided an excellent clinical picture of adult addiction, as may occur in alcoholism or other chemical dependencies.

Anyone familiar with alcoholism will immediately recognize the pattern, and if one substitutes "alcohol" or "food" for "blanket," the series of cartoons that follows would make an excellent primer on alcoholism, drug addiction, or compulsive eating. Much of the data can be applied to addictive interpersonal relationships as well, as we will see in a subsequent chapter.

This has its counterpart in the enormous resistance to treatment that is manifest when an addict is confronted with his problem and realizes that treatment will require giving up the addictive object or behavior, a thought that generates intense anxiety.

People in the environment of the addict may become very critical of the addictive behavior, and the addict may not be able to understand why they do not appreciate the value of the object (blanket, food, alcohol) as he does. To him, the object has such great functional value that he feels that everyone should appreciate it in at least some way.

Clinical experience has proven that pointing out the destructive aspects of the addiction, such as the serious health hazards of alcohol, drugs, or excessive food, makes no impression whatever on the addict, who has a delusion of immunity. The addict is incapable of believing he can be affected; it simply does not apply to him.

People often wonder why the addict cannot see the ultimate consequences of the addiction. However, alcoholics know that their continued drinking is likely to result in life-threatening liver disease, cocaine and heroin users are aware of the risk of sudden death and AIDS, and smokers invariably know that cigarette smoking leads to cancer, emphysema, and heart disease. So why do they continue their addiction?

The answer, as I pointed out in my book *Addictive Thinking*, is that the addict's concept of time is much different from that of the nonaddict. The addict thinks in terms of seconds, minutes, and sometimes hours. The "future," as most people understand it, is not within the addict's scope of thinking. Hence, anything that will occur at some later time has no bearing whatsoever on the addict's behavior.

Linus thinks that anyone who objects to his blanket is a fanatic, just as the alcoholic thinks anyone who objects to his drinking is an evangelist on a temperance kick, which is more than enough reason to dismiss their opinions as being without merit.

As in the case cited of the young man who was rejected by his

girlfriend (p. 76) or as in the case of an alcoholic who has
exhausted his supply of alcohol, nothing will stand in the
addict's way of retrieving the object.

Social relationships are often ruined by alcoholism. The
alcoholic may offend people without realizing it, or his behavior
may be so embarrassing that people do not want to be in his
company. When it is pointed out to the alcoholic that even his
best friends want nothing to do with him, he invariably forgoes
the friendships in favor of the alcohol on which he has become
so dependent.

Efforts by family or friends to bring the addiction to an end
may result in promises that are never kept. The addict may go
through the motions of surrendering the object of the addiction,
but it is evident that he has no intention of actually doing so.

Spouses of alcoholics frequently try to control the addiction
by hiding bottles or, better yet, pouring the liquor down the
drain. However, for every bottle the spouse discards, the alcoholic has two others stashed away safely in the garage, attic, or
basement. Visitors to the home of Dr. Bob (one of the two

co-founders of Alcoholics Anonymous) in Akron, Ohio, are shown the hiding places where he used to conceal his bottles. The bottles the spouse discards are probably meant to be found, and probably contain water or tea rather than alcohol, because the latter is closely guarded.

The alcoholic's capacity to rationalize is virtually limitless. One alcoholic, an executive who had been adamant in his refusal to admit his problem, was finally confronted by his family and friends en masse, and reluctantly agreed to submit to an evaluation. In his interview with me, he stated he was grateful that so many people cared about his health and welfare, and he would now indeed curtail his use of alcohol.

I pointed out that whereas his intentions were noble, there was no way he could successfully achieve abstinence without help, and I suggested several treatment options. His response was that he could not accept treatment because inasmuch as he was certain that he could stop drinking on his own, accepting treatment when it was unnecessary *would be dishonest.*

This man had not spoken the truth for years, having consistently

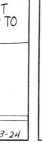

lied to cover up his derelictions consequent to his drinking. Yet now he was refusing treatment because of his *dedication to honesty.* Alcoholics frequently rationalize and may delude themselves that they are actually acting in everyone's best interest.

If the addict does abstain (from alcohol, food, or drugs) for even the briefest period of time, he is likely to consider himself cured and expects to be congratulated for his achievement. Yet the alcoholic is apt to relapse to surreptitious drinking even while trying to convince others that he is indeed abstaining.

Typically, the addict rejects help and insists on doing it by himself.

If the addict can consider four minutes of abstinence a resounding success, imagine what he thinks an entire weekend of abstinence to be! While we do not wish to deprive Linus of his elation, considering oneself "cured" because of forty-eight hours' abstinence is a bit premature. But to Linus, the ego trip of having accomplished this without external help distorts his perspective. During the active addiction, the addict is con-

cerned only with the immediate gratification and totally dismisses the future. Similarly, in early recovery, the addict may be unaware of the minuscule duration of the abstinence, equating a weekend with a lifetime.

Filled with pride over his triumph, the addict becomes a missionary for the cause, aggressively trying to win others over to his newfound happiness.

Linus may find his noble efforts to help others to be rather unwelcome.

In response, Linus retreats to a more passive role. He will still share his triumph with others, but they must now come to him for help.

Addicts like things to happen fast. Alcohol and drugs give them an instantaneous "high"; so when they finally give up their addiction, they may want an instantaneous recovery. In fact, some may become instantaneous specialists.

As anyone familiar with addiction knows, most clients do not come to treatment willingly. They are generally coerced either by family, employer, or the court. Consequently, even the feeblest of excuses reinforces their resistance and suffices for them to try to leave treatment.

Schulz portrays a common fallacy of psychotherapy for addiction—namely, trying to understand the reason behind the addiction. Experience has demonstrated that this approach is generally ineffective. Treatment of a destructive addiction is much like trying to extinguish a destructive fire. One must first douse the fire, and only when this has been accomplished is it appropriate to look for its cause. Trying to understand why a person drinks before the alcohol is curtailed can be as unwise as trying to discover what caused a fire before it has been extinguished.

Even when the addict provides reasons for his habit, these are usually rationalizations and not the true causes. Lucy may be on the right track, because whatever reasons one may give to justify the addiction, the fact is that it is invariably self-destructive, and it is simply stupid to do something that is self-destructive.

The shallow quality of Linus's recovery is likely to give way under the least stress, resulting in a relapse.

Just as the addict may seek to blame others for his addiction, he also blames everyone else for his relapse.

An important component in addiction is the phenomenon of "enabling." People in the environment of the addict may try to help, but they are likely to be unaware that their help may actually be contributing to the addiction.

As in the fire analogy, while the cause may indeed be the match that ignited it, the fire can burn only in the presence of oxygen. While no one in the addict's environment may be the "cause" of the addiction, some people provide the "oxygen" that allows it to persist.

Things may get bad enough so that the addict seeks help. Surprisingly, some people who complain loudest about the addiction are the least helpful in recovery.

In the addiction treatment field, we speak of "enablers" or "co-dependents." These are people who are close to the addict who may have hang-ups of their own that feed into the addiction.

Indeed, whereas the addict may have his or her thought processes impaired by the chemical, the behavior of the "enabler," who is functioning with an unimpaired brain, may be more difficult to comprehend.

When the substitute for the transitional object is a person rather than alcohol or drugs, the result is the development of an "addictive relationship." Let us look at this in the next chapter.

7

Addictive Relationships

*I*t is not uncommon these days, when so many things are referred to as being addictive, to hear the term *addictive relationship.*

What exactly is an addictive relationship? It is perhaps best defined by comparing it to the prototype of addictions: alcoholism. There we see that a person is *addicted* to alcohol because he insists on drinking it even in the face of incontrovertible evidence that he should stop. We may, therefore, say that a relationship can be considered "addictive" when a person insists on continuing it even in the face of evidence that he should let it go.

The most prominent symptom of alcohol addiction is *denial,* whereby the alcoholic obstinately refuses to accept the reality that he cannot use alcohol. In the addictive relationship, the affected individual steadfastly denies the reality that he cannot have the object of his desire.

One young man who came for a psychiatric evaluation stated that he had just been rejected by his girlfriend, and he admitted that he had been both verbally and physically abusive to her. He stated that if she did not reconsider and reinstate their relationship he would kill himself, and he begged that I call her and intervene on his behalf and convey his sincere promise that he would never again repeat his abusive behavior. He was terribly disappointed at my refusal to do as he asked.

During the next week he called me several times a day, crying and begging me to intervene for him. He said that his girlfriend had changed her telephone number to an unlisted one and I would have to reach her through her parents. When I again refused, he then waited for her outside her home, followed her to work, and was ultimately arrested for harassment. Whereas many people react to a severed relationship with an appropriate measure of grief, this young man's behavior was clearly of an addictive nature.

While it may be difficult to pinpoint precise causes for the development of an addictive relationship, some of the factors we noted earlier may be operative.

We have seen that Lucy is really a very insecure person. She felt threatened by a younger sibling who displaced her, at least partially, as the focus of parental love and attention. To compensate for the feeling of being rejected, Lucy developed an attitude of grandiosity. These two factors—the need to be loved and believing that one is the greatest—set the stage for the development of an addictive relationship.

In Lucy's case, it was a crush on Schroeder.

Although Schroeder makes it abundantly clear to Lucy that he has no romantic interest whatever in her, Lucy simply refuses to take "no" for an answer.

The similarity to alcohol addiction is further evident in the phenomenon of rationalization. Just as an alcoholic will provide ingenious reasons as to why he needs the alcohol, a person in an addictive relationship will use all possible means to convince the other person why the relationship should continue.

Lucy was rather successful in achieving dominance over her younger sibling and controlling him. She now tries to control Schroeder as well. The subject in the addictive relationship may try to ingratiate him- or herself with the other person and may not realize that such efforts can be counterproductive.

Sometimes he or she may try to appeal to the other person's conscience.

We have already seen that guilt can be a very powerful tool, and this is often used to try to maintain the relationship.

People with deep feelings of inferiority may be so starved for any sign of affirmation that they may actually interpret derogatory comments as indications of appreciation.

Certainly Schroeder doesn't intend a handful of crabgrass to be a bouquet, but given Lucy's fragile self-image, that is precisely how she interprets it, and uses it as evidence of his affection for her.

Needless to say, if even derogatory comments are interpreted favorably, just imagine how the slightest positive comment can be magnified to meet one's needs. In relating to someone with such a pattern, one must be extremely cautious about what one says. A statement that was intended to be simply a polite

compliment may be misinterpreted as an iron-clad commitment.

The addict may try to use authority figures to convince the other person to accept him, as did the young man who pleaded for me to intervene with his girlfriend. The addict may attempt to exploit the other person's parents, teachers, clergy, or anyone else he thinks may change the other person's mind.

We have already seen how guilt can be utilized to manipulate others; a person in an addictive relationship may try to make the other person feel guilty for acts of omission as well as acts of commission.

Lucy manifests her underlying feelings of *inferiority* when she glorifies a handful of crabgrass, yet, on the other hand, she continues to assert her attitude of *superiority*. In the addictive relationship, these conflicting attitudes can co-exist.

The similarity between addiction to alcohol or cocaine and the addiction to a person can be striking. In either case, the addicted person refuses to surrender the object of the addiction regardless of the most convincing arguments to that effect.

Many alcohol-addicted people, even if they reluctantly accept the fact that they cannot use alcohol, may see this as only a temporary restriction. They may harbor the hope that sometime

in the future they will again be able to drink safely.

Although the object of the affection may try to make it perfectly clear that he or she does not feel the same way, the

addict will nevertheless continue to believe that she or he is in fact appreciated and desired.

The addict may try to convince the other person that rejection will cause the addict to go insane, thereby appealing to the object's compassion as well as utilizing guilt.

When the addict becomes desperate, he or she may threaten to commit suicide if not accepted. The addict fails to see that such manipulations are counterproductive, since most people would not wish to enter into a relationship where they would always be at the mercy of someone's suicidal threats.

I have often observed spouses and lovers visiting a rejected partner in the hospital after the latter had made a suicidal gesture. In all these cases, the addict feels that he or she has scored a point or two and is shocked to discover that the gesture did not have the desired effect.

In addictive relationships, as in chemical addiction, there are co-dependents—that is, people who strenuously object to the addict's drinking or drugging yet somehow contribute to the

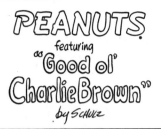

SOMETIMES I THINK YOU DON'T REALIZE THAT YOU COULD LOSE ME...

2-24

ARE YOU SURE YOU WANT TO SUFFER THE TORTURES OF THE MEMORY OF A LOST LOVE?

DO YOU KNOW THE TORTURES OF THE MEMORY OF A LOST LOVE?

IT'S AWFUL!!!

IT WILL HAUNT YOU NIGHT AND DAY!!

YOU'LL WAKE UP AT NIGHT SCREAMING!

YOU CAN'T EAT! YOU CAN'T SLEEP!! YOU'LL WANT TO SMASH THINGS!

YOU'LL HATE YOURSELF AND THE WORLD AND EVERYBODY IN IT!

OOOOoo!!!

ARE YOU SURE YOU WANT TO RISK LOSING ME?

addiction. I have often heard the wife of an alcoholic state that although she had vehemently objected to her husband's drinking, she had even greater difficulty in adjusting to his abstinence. It is as though the alcohol, repulsive as it may have been, had become so much a part of the daily routine that she felt an uneasiness when it was no longer there!

Although Schroeder has made it clear that he does not want any part of Lucy, his reaction to her leaving is quite typical of the co-dependent.

As annoying as Lucy may have been, she nevertheless became an integral part of Schroeder's reality. Although he may not have loved her, life without Lucy could be rather boring.

Lucy may thus not have been completely wrong in assuming that Schroeder had some positive feelings for her. Schroeder tries to explain that he did not intend his negative remarks to Lucy to be insults. Not infrequently we may see this type of communication between a couple. An exchange of barbs that may appear to be a hostile exchange is actually their way of expressing care for each other. This is, however, not a satisfactory method of demonstrating affection, even if it is accepted by both partners. One can never tell when a caustic remark that

was intended to be benign strikes a tender nerve and elicits pain.

Of all possible scenes, Schroeder conjures up what we might have thought to be the least likely fantasy—namely, that he might actually marry Lucy.

Some dependent–co-dependent relationships may be of long duration, since, in some ways, each person may fulfill some of the partner's needs. The relationship, however, is apt to be tenuous, and can disintegrate when one of two things occur: (1) the dependent person's negative behavior exceeds the tolerance or needs of the co-dependent, or (2) the co-dependent becomes healthier and no longer has the needs the dependent was satisfying.

The example cited by no means exhausts the phenomenon of the addictive relationship. Just as the varieties of alcoholism or other addictions are legion, so it is with relationships.

But this is where the analogy to alcohol and drugs stops. Whereas addiction to alcohol or other harmful chemicals must be curtailed, this does not necessarily apply to addictive relationships. People can grow and change, and it is possible to build on the positive aspects of a relationship and eliminate the negative factors. With proper help, which may require the expertise of a counselor, an addictive relationship may be converted into a true loving one.

8

Love

Mature love is a relationship between two people wherein each partner both gives affection and feels capable and entitled to receive that affection. While this may appear elementary, there are some relationships that may be thought of as "loving" yet this simply does not occur.

For example, in an addictive relationship, the exchange is markedly skewed toward the receiving aspect, because the addicted partner is so intent on receiving that he or she gives little or nothing to the relationship. In fact, the addicted partner may not even be affected by the fact that the other partner is irritated with him or her. The emphasis is totally on what can be taken out of the relationship rather than what can be put in.

At the other end of the spectrum is the person who may not feel capable of entering or sustaining a relationship because he or she does not feel worthy of receiving affection. This person is more than ready to give, but may feel that any attempt at doing so would be repelled because the other person would not be interested in what is being offered. When people like this enter into a relationship, they may be distrustful of the other's love because they feel they do not deserve it. They may also exhaust themselves in trying to do things for the other person in order to compensate for their being "stuck" with so inadequate a partner as themselves.

Charlie Brown is an example of a person who considers himself unlovable. He has fallen in love with the little red-haired girl, but Charlie's self-esteem is so low that he does not think it possible that the little girl would even acknowledge his existence.

How crucial is the role of self-esteem can be demonstrated by the following case. A young woman consulted me because of her concern that her marriage was deteriorating. Her husband had recently undergone a marked personality change, having become extremely irascible and verbally abusive, and although she loved him very much, she did not feel she could continue in the relationship under those circumstances.

Frank earned a comfortable living as a home builder. He and Evelyn had been married for seventeen years and had four children. When their youngest child was old enough to attend school a full day, Evelyn found herself with free time and took some courses to obtain a realtor's license. It was when she began to earn commissions on the homes she sold that Frank's demeanor toward her changed drastically. He began to forbid her to go out evenings to show homes to prospective buyers, even accusing her of philandering. He insisted that she stay home on weekends, accusing her of deserting her children when she went out to meet clients.

A study of the case revealed that whereas they had enjoyed an apparently excellent relationship, Frank had always been insecure about Evelyn's love for him. His self-esteem was so poor that he thought of himself as being unlovable. He often wondered why Evelyn had married him and why she had stayed in the marriage, and concluded that the only positive aspect she could see in him was economic security. If this were so, then if she became economically self-sufficient there would be no reason for her to remain with him. He therefore saw her newly acquired earning capacity as extremely threatening.

Fortunately, appropriate therapy helped Frank to a self-awareness and an improved self-esteem, which allowed him to accept Evelyn's love and preserved a marriage that was otherwise in danger of disintegrating.

*L*inus tells Charlie that his feelings of worthlessness are unwarranted, and that Charlie feels this way only because he is depressed. From a clinical point of view, Linus may be quite correct. Even people with good self-esteem may feel completely negative about themselves when in a state of depression. We might then assume that when Charlie's depressed mood passes, he will feel differently about himself and then be able to strike up a relationship with the little red-haired girl. Sometimes Charlie does begin to think that perhaps this is indeed possible. The little red-haired girl may have actually noticed him, and may even want to meet him.

But alas! Charlie's hopes are dashed.

Although Charlie may not feel so severely depressed as to think that his very existence is not even noticed, he still does

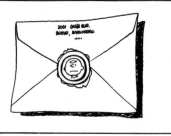

not think he has much of a chance of attracting the little red-haired girl. He is hesitant to try for fear of failure. As we have seen earlier, Snoopy escapes into fantasy when he is dissatisfied with reality. Charlie, too, allays his frustration by a flight into fantasy where his hopes are realized.

Like Snoopy, Charlie eventually comes back to what he sees as his reality.

Charlie recognizes that his reluctance to approach the little red-haired girl is due to his self-deprecation, but does not see any way out. He therefore resigns himself to the inevitable, and decides that he can go on with life without the cherished object of his love. In order to do so, however, he would have to repress his feelings, because otherwise the frustration would paralyze him. Unfortunately, Charlie's repressive defenses do not work well.

The failure to put the little red-haired girl out of his mind does indeed affect Charlie to the point where others begin to notice it. Peppermint Patty calls Charlie's attention to this, and Charlie realizes that he is on the horns of a dilemma: He is

unable to relate to the little girl but is also unable to forget her.

This dilemma is a common occurrence in adults and may have far-reaching effects. People with this problem may not be able to relate to the objects of their love, but they may also not be able to detach in order to develop other love relationships.

Charlie might be using his inability to detach himself from the little red-haired girl to avoid making new relationships. People who lack self-confidence and hesitate to try new ventures for fear of failing may not be able to see that this anxiety is their primary problem. Instead, they attribute their paralysis to their inability to get over a rejection. They not only believe this themselves, but they also convince their psychotherapists that they are in a depressed state because of this rejection. They spend hours in therapy trying to resolve the feelings of rejection, but this is totally futile, because the true reason for their inability to progress is not in the pain of the past but rather in the fear of the future.

As a child, I was not permitted to go boating unaccompanied

by an adult. Inasmuch as I loved to row, I would sit in a boat that was tethered to the pier and row away to my heart's content. There was no danger of my going into the midst of the lake because the boat was securely tied to the pier.

Similarly, people who fear the future may "tether" themselves to an event or events of the past. Many patients have deceived their therapists as well as themselves in attributing their stagnation to childhood traumas or romantic rejections when in fact it is the fear of the future that is the real culprit.

Peppermint Patty is aware that Charlie Brown's problem involves the future at least as much as it does the past, and Charlie indeed confirms this.

Marriages built on a need to "mother" a spouse may be precarious. When such a couple starts having children, the woman may be exhausted by the constant drain on her energies; she could now use a husband who is supportive and willing to share in the responsibilities of caring for the family rather than

one who desires mothering himself. These women often say, "I don't have a husband and two children to care for. I have *three* children."

Ideally, people close to those who exhibit this aspect of Charlie Brown's personality should encourage them to get counseling and build their self-esteem so that they can enter into a mature romantic relationship on an equal footing. If, however, they do not hold these people in high-esteem, they might well encourage them to accept a maternal type of love, perhaps because they consider them incapable of achieving a more mature one.

Sally, as we have seen in a previous chapter, does not give her brother high ratings, thinks that he should be thrilled by the fact that someone likes him, and should take advantage of this opportunity.

The more pathetic Charlie Brown appears to be, the more he arouses Marci's maternal instinct.

Marci's comment "He made me so mad, I told him I liked him" might seem rather confusing.

Although hostility and affection appear to be polar opposites and hence mutually exclusive, there is really no such incompatibility when parents have these feelings toward their children. Parents can have intense love for their children yet be very angry at them. Indeed, parents sometimes seem to manifest the greatest degree of love for children who incite them the most.

This is often encountered in treatment of addicted youngsters. One might think that the aggravation the children cause their parents would make it easier for the parents to adopt the recommended "tough love" attitude. Yet much to everyone's surprise, parents often take a very protective attitude toward the children who cause them the greatest distress! It is not unusual for the healthier and better-behaved children to make this observation, and there is, of course, the danger that these children will conclude that if deviant behavior is rewarded by parental caring, that must be the thing to do.

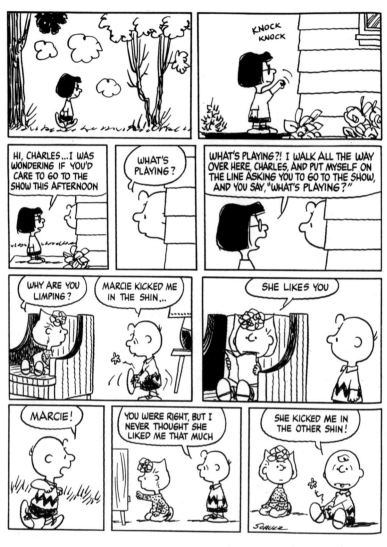

This is not a new phenomenon. Students of the Bible will recall how Absalom, King David's son, revolted against his father and sought to kill him. David gave strict orders to his generals to be certain not to harm Absalom, and when he learned that his son was killed in battle, the grieving father wept bitterly for his defiant son, saying, "My son, my son! Would that I had died in your place." (Samuel II, 19:1)

One of the problems with this type of love relationship is that being treated like a child can evoke not only maternal *love* but also maternal *discipline*. Indeed, if one accepts a maternal type of love, one must be prepared to accept all aspects of a mother-child relationship. Men who enter this type of relationship, however, are likely to refuse to pay the price of being spanked when they do not behave like the nice little boy Mommy expects them to be.

Charlie has another admirer, Peppermint Patty, who happens to be an excellent athlete and is thus far superior to Charlie, who loses every ball game. Patty's attraction to Charlie is a result of her own poor self-image. This, too, can become a basis for a relationship, and among adults we often find relationships where partners are attracted to each other because neither has the hope of being loved by anyone better.

Patty can only hint to Charlie Brown that she is fond of him. Because she feels she is unattractive, she anticipates that a more open declaration of her feelings for him will be answered with rejection, especially since she knows that Charlie has not yet completely forgotten the little red-haired girl.

Patty is extremely conscious of her appearance, and although Charlie Brown assures her that she is lovable, or at least will be so in the future, Patty interprets his "sure" to refer to her unattractiveness rather than to her being lovable. When presented with two possibilities, people with poor self-esteem will consistently interpret comments about themselves in a negative light.

Marci and Patty are both fond of Charlie Brown. Marci offers him a maternal type of love. She can do this because even though she does not think of herself as beautiful, she does know that she is intelligent, and having this feeling of self-worth, she is not terrified by a possible rejection. Furthermore, a characteristic of maternal love is that mothers seem to be undaunted when their love for their children is not reciprocated.

Patty, on the other hand, does not offer a maternal type of love. On the contrary, she competes with Charlie Brown in athletics, which is of great importance to him, and totally demolishes him. The one area in which she does not feel inferior is precisely the one she cannot use to attract him. Hence, Patty is left with no reason to expect her affection to be reciprocated.

Nevertheless, Patty tries to soften the impact of her athletic superiority. Knowing how enraptured Charlie Brown is by baseball, she appeals to his ideology, as if to say, "If you cannot appreciate me in the concrete, you may be able to appreciate me in the abstract."

Patty follows through with a philosophical discussion, hoping, perhaps, to elicit some sympathy from Charlie Brown. If he cannot have love for her based upon her attractiveness, he

might at least have a modicum of love for her based upon feeling sorry for her. Patty therefore exaggerates her defects, hoping Charlie might say, "Your nose really isn't all that ugly." This would at least be a partial victory.

However, that is not to be. Charlie Brown does not take the bait.

Marci is much more benign than Patty, and perhaps for this reason Charlie responds to Marci. He still holds the torch for his little red-haired girl, so his response to Marci is more platonic than romantic. Patty, however, does not see it this way. She is offended and becomes jealous.

Jealousy is sometimes mistaken for love. A jealous lover may go to all extremes, including risking his very life, to repel anyone who represents even a remote threat to his exclusive rights to his "beloved."

But is this really love? Just a bit of analysis will reveal that this is possessiveness not love, and the jealous lover is protecting his own interest rather than exhibiting true love for the other person.

Some partners in a relationship are initially very flattered by jealousy, and they interpret the possessiveness as an indication of how highly they are valued. Invariably, this initial pride of being so highly prized leads to feelings of resentment as one becomes aware that the dynamic at work is not love but narcissism. It is not that the jealous partner loves the other person, but that he loves himself so intensely.

Peppermint Patty initially expresses her jealousy as love, but in the single frame where Charles Schulz has Patty angrily cross out "love," he teaches us the true nature of jealousy. It is anything but love.

We have thus seen several types of attitudes and reactions that can occur among children, and it is only logical to assume that unless something occurs to modify these, they will become the bases for adult relationships that are likely to be quite problematic. At the very least, we might become aware of how devastating a low self-esteem can be to the development of a mature love relationship. People with positive self-esteem will feel that

the love they have to offer is of value, and that they are deserving of receiving love. They are less likely to enter into relationships where there is a marked disparity between partners, such as a parent-child relationship. They are not apt to interpret everything relating to themselves as negative, and are unlikely to have the narcissism that results in jealousy.

9

Power

While some of our drives may wax and wane as we go through life, one seems to be fairly consistent, and that is the lust for power. Already in prenursery one can observe the development of a pecking-order, and this pattern persists throughout adult life and well into the senior years. Some people manage to attain positions of power, but even those who become subordinates may do so only because they feel they are unable to achieve a superior position rather than because they do not desire it. Should the opportunity present itself, the meek, passive individual may indeed manifest a lust for power.

What is behind this drive for power? There may be nothing behind it. It may indeed be a primary drive, much like hunger, thirst, or sex. It may not necessarily be a quest for recognition or adoration by others, as is evident when people seek power over others who are unable to acknowledge anyone's superiority.

Strangely, Lucy is unable to see that she is manifesting the very attitude of superiority that she is condemning in others.

The intensity of the attraction of power is evident in the

sacrifices some people are willing to make to achieve it. Some people forgo lucrative salaries in order to take positions of authority, even though it provides them with significantly less income. Some people who live in relative comfort have sought high governmental positions that are often thankless jobs, laden with complaints from disgruntled constituents, and have sacrificed the relative security of private life, placing themselves at greater risk of danger from adversaries and even exposing themselves to assassination. They have relinquished their privacy, placing themselves at the mercy of the media, whose sensation-seeking reporters may try to dredge up every conceivable indiscretion of one's past. That people nevertheless pursue positions of power attests to its inordinate lure.

As we have seen, Lucy is one who seeks dominion, even if only over bugs. Being in a position of authority over peers would certainly be much more gratifying, but Lucy is aware that she may lack the popularity to be elected to office.

Since Lucy cannot achieve this position herself, she becomes a "kingmaker," a phenomenon not unknown among adults, wherein one asserts authority via a "puppet" candidate. The only person she can find to put up for office is Linus. But alas! Linus shows no signs of ambition. When things do not go his way, Linus simply retreats to the comfort of his thumb and blanket. Linus is hardly presidential material.

But Lucy is clever. The lure for power can transform even the meekest individual into a fierce contender.

Although Linus has some misgivings about the job he soon overcomes these and becomes very assertive. Indeed, the meek Linus even hints at doing away with the democratic process and becoming a dictator!

Kingmakers are occasionally surprised to discover that they may not be in total control of their candidate, whose ambition may have gone to his head, and who may now resist being manipulated, insisting on making his own decisions.

Why do candidates whose defeat appears to be forgone conclusion cling to the hope that they will triumph? Because people often believe what they want to believe.

Can the lure of power really alter one's personality? Just look at what has happened to the person who had previously reacted

to striking out by retreating to his thumb and blanket! It does not take long for a candidate to realize that he must appeal to a broad spectrum of voters. He may be unable to understand why anyone, except perhaps his opponent's family and close friends, would not support him.

Probably nothing is so terrifying to a candidate's support team as the thought that their standard-bearer might make a remark that will make him the butt of ridicule. All the laborious effort invested in a campaign is at risk of being undone by a single foolish comment.

To the very end, the candidate may feel obligated to promote the values he espouses, even if doing so results in his defeat. His support team, who have been denied the spoils of office, are usually totally unsympathetic to the candidate's idealism.

The candidate may take his case to the public, insisting that championing one's values is a virtue that supersedes all other considerations. Most people are likely to be rather indifferent to his cause, but pragmatists have learned a lesson: evangelism for unpopular causes is not likely to bring in many votes.

What about the candidate's continued loyalty to his cherished values? Well, having sacrificed so much for them, he is likely to remain faithful to his cause. But even the most ardent devotee may have a breaking point.

For example, we have witnessed hundreds of millions of people dedicated to Communist doctrine for more than half a century, but when the system ultimately failed to deliver on its promises, it was discarded even by some of its most zealous champions.

Let us, however, rethink the premise stated at the outset of this chapter—namely, that the drive for power is primary, like hunger, thirst, or sex. That may not be completely true.

In *When Do the Good Things Start?*, I discussed the role of self-esteem in human behavior, and noted that people who feel themselves to be inadequate may react in any one of a number of ways, either surrendering to these feelings or trying to deny them in one way or another.

Perhaps the drive for power is just another way to overcome intolerable feelings of inadequacy. This may be the reason why

some people will give up so much in order to attain power. They are willing to pay the price to relieve themselves of the distressful feelings of worthlessness.

If this is true, we can spare ourselves much stress by ridding ourselves of unwarranted feelings of inadequacy. How can this be achieved? There are some suggestions in *Waking Up Just in Time*. Other methods of achieving self-awareness may also be helpful, but it is first necessary to realize that groundless assumptions of inadequacy are at the root of many of our problems. If we can only discover that we are really much better than we think we are, we may be able to enjoy a happier and more productive life.

Epilogue

Virtually all schools of psychology place great emphasis on the experiences of childhood and how they influence adult behavior. Some refer to "the child within us," implying that we may never actually outgrow childhood, and that maturation often consists of building an adult enclosure, or "shell," at the center of which resides the child with all juvenile emotions intact. Problems in living may arise when this childish core tries to break the adult "shell."

The overwhelming majority of our adult lives is spent in interpersonal relationships: family, friends, society as a whole. Here, too, the behavior appropriate for an adult may be at odds with the desires and fears of the child within. When such conflicts occur, a person may seek various ways to resolve them.

But what happens when the adult "shell," instead of being an enclosure comprised of maturation, is itself fashioned after juvenile behavior? Then we have a childish core and a shell that is not much more mature than the force within. This may actually make for greater compatibility within the individual, who is thus not caught up in an internal conflict, but it can certainly result in major difficulties with a society that expects mature behavior and is not very tolerant of an adult who acts like a child.

Charles Schulz gives us some precious insights into some of the sources of such maladjustments. Our adult interpersonal relationships may be, to a great degree, shaped by juvenile interpersonal relationships. The better we can understand the latter, the better equipped we are to lessen the impact on the former, particularly when such impact is detrimental to our well-being.

We owe a debt of gratitude to the creator of Charlie Brown, Lucy, Linus, Snoopy, and their friends for helping us understand ourselves a bit better.

Insightful Advice from Abraham J. Twerski, M.D.,
and Charles M. Schulz

When Do the Good Things Start?

Dr. Twerski provides a down-to-earth self-help guide to personal problem-solving by using Charles M. Schulz's beloved *Peanuts*® cartoons to offer guidance and insight on dealing with the problems of everyday life. *128 pages, Illustrated, Paperback, $7.95*

Waking Up Just in Time

Using the Twelve Steps approach employed successfully for decades by such groups as Alcoholics Anonymous, Dr. Twerski uses *Peanuts* comic strips to show how this approach can be applied to overcoming any problem life might offer.

128 pages, Illustrated, Paperback, $7.95

I Didn't Ask to Be in This Family

Twerski and Schulz team up again to explore sibling rivalries and relationships and to offer advice on overcoming the problems of early behavior patterns that can affect us for the rest of our lives.

128 pages, Illustrated, Paperback, $7.95

Please send me:

_____ copies of *When Do The Good Things Start?* @ $7.95 each

_____ copies of *Waking Up Just In Time* @ $7.95 each

_____ copies of *I Didn't Ask to Be in This Family* @ $7.95 each

Please include $1.50 per book ordered for shipping and handling.

Name _____

Address _____

City _____ State_____ Zip _____

Please enclose a check or money order payable to Pharos Books and send to: Pharos Books, Sales Department, 200 Park Avenue, New York, NY, 10166.